Four C Dell'Arte Plays with Stage Directions

By

Irene Mawer

British Library Cataloguing-in-Publication Data
A catalogue record for this book is available from
the British Library

THE PIERROTS AT VERSAILLES

*(Music selected from the works of
Schumann and F. Swinstead.)*

The play has been performed at the Arts Theatre, the Rudolf Steiner Hall, at pastoral performances at Stratford-on-Avon and Malvern, and in the Ginner-Mawer Performances in Hyde Park under the auspices of the League of Arts, 1930, 1931.

The original cast was as follows :

Pierrot Blanc	*Irene Mawer*
Pierrot Noir	*Joyce Ruscoe*
Madame la Marquise	*Lesley Hodson*
Monsieur le Marquis	*Evelyn Doak*
The Negro Servant	*Margaret Rubel*
Jeunes Filles	{ *Mary Wardrop* { *Kathleen Scott*

The play was in all instances produced by the author.

THE PIERROTS AT VERSAILLES

The moon shines upon the Gardens of Versailles. The shadows are full of mystery, the glades are wonder-lit, for we are in the eighteenth century, when every lady was a poem, perfect in form, from her high-heeled shoes to the rosebud hidden under the topmost curl of her elaborate coiffure. The gardens and the ladies are such as Watteau knew, and he has shown us that where there are lovely ladies among the trees, there is almost sure to be the wondering, wide-eyed figure of a Pierrot, bringing into the conventional atmosphere of the Court the childlike simplicity of the peasant. Here, then, are ladies, one especially exquisite, and two Pierrots, each white-faced, but one dressed in black, the other in white. Where there is a lady we may be sure there is a lord, so the characters are :

Pierrot Blanc
Pierrot Noir
Madame la Marquise
Monsieur le Marquis
Jeunes Filles
A Negro Servant

The Scene is a glade in the Gardens with a terrace at the back, beyond which burns the night sky. Against the sky are silhouetted two formal trees. Down right is a stone seat. The light of the full moon makes everything as clear as day, yet more romantic.

A.　From among the shadows, up left, flit two moth-like figures ; they are the Jeunes Filles, little ladies-in-waiting upon Madame la Marquise. They float into the moonlight, rest for a moment down left, their heads, crowned with rose-wreaths, laid close together, for the exchange of some piece of delicious scandal. Then they are away again, up to the back, where two fingers laid on two pairs of lips hush back the little gurgles of mischief we half expect to hear, as out from the darkness drifts the exquisite figure of la Marquise herself. She has wandered into the gardens, half in love with the beauty of the night, to enjoy the romantic experience of reading a book of poems by moonlight. As she passes on, the little girls slip away out of sight, and she is left alone in the glade and the moonlight.

What a picture! The beautiful lady, the moonlight, the shadowed trees ; and how well she knows that she perfectly befits this perfect moment.

She drifts like some stately galleon down left, crosses to the seat, glances at the book, wanders up to the terrace, and, at last, floats away once more, to other moonlit spaces, leaving our picture empty of all save the memory of her, that is like the sound of some old minuet played gravely, but with a haunting sweetness.

B.   Only for a moment is the picture empty, for hardly has la Marquise disappeared, than a white figure steals on from up right. It is Pierrot Blanc, afraid of the shadows, afraid of the moon, afraid of the stately, courtly place, but drawn by the vision of the sweet face of the Marquise as he saw it when he watched her unseen. In his arms is a sheaf of white lilies. Somehow he must find her and lay them at her feet, and declare to her the passion that stirs under his white coat. He tiptoes with long, cautious steps across the back ; then turns in a panic, to find his own shadow following him. He retreats to the safety of the trees whence he came. Once more he cautiously reaches the centre of the terrace, where he stands gazing in the direction in which the Marquise disappeared. His back is to the audience, so he fails to see, as we do, another white face appear. This time it is down left, and cautiously, cautiously Pierrot Noir crawls out from the bushes, also in terror of the night, yet drawn on by the irresistible vision of the Marquise. He carries with infinite care the poem which he will lay at her feet when at last he meets her and can tell her of the love that burns under his black coat. He crawls to the centre front, then darts back again into the shadows. Again he creeps forward, this time right across the front to the opposite proscenium, where he remains peering into the shadows, for unknown dangers, or wondering which way his vision really disappeared.

Now Pierrot Blanc begins to move again. This time he tiptoes to up left and peers between the trees. Each Pierrot thinks he sees some one coming, and, with desperate care, retreats backwards towards the centre. They hold their breaths ; every step is anxiously taken. Till, horror ! each meets some unknown person with a sickening bump. Ghosts ! Gendarmes ! Fire ! Murder !

Without stopping to see with what they have collided, they dart away into the shadows by the proscenium, Pierrot Blanc down left, Pierrot Noir down right. They hide their terrified eyes against the tree-trunks (which are the proscenium as we see it). Slowly, as nothing further happens, they each peer out. There is a suspicious form over there. Ghost ? Gendarme ? No ! Frère Pierrot ! A thousand thunders ! The intruder, the base spoil-sport ! Courage returns with rage. Each says simultaneously (they have a maddening habit of saying the same thing at the same moment), ' You ! '

Enraged and dignified they advance towards each other. They stand together, centre, the picture of two naughty children playing at being outraged heroes of romance.

C.   Pierrot Noir, with dignity, inquires, ' You here ? Why ? ' Pierrot Blanc coldly answers, ' *You* here ? Why ? ' Pierrot Noir says emphatically, ' You go away.' Pierrot Blanc replies, ' On the contrary, I shall stay just here.' Then they speak together, ' You and I, why are we here, anyway ? ' And with a knowing look they answer themselves, ' The exquisite lady walks here, that's why.' Then Pierrot Noir, as one settling the question for ever, says, ' I have written this perfect poem for her.' But Pierrot Blanc merely replies with a greater flourish, ' And I have brought her these most exquisite lilies.' Together they sigh in ecstatic fervour, ' I *adore* her ! '

Their gesture is superb. Their fears are gone. The moonlight shines on two small forms transfigured and tense with emotion.

D.   But hark ! Some one is coming. Their heroics collapse.

Once more two terrified figures dash for the proscenium trees, as a delicate little air steals into our ears, and into our sight there floats again the figure of one of the girls. She is followed almost immediately by the Negro *laquais*, then by the Marquise herself, followed by the second girl. The Marquise reclines on the seat and bids the girls settle on the grass beside her. And there they are, just like some Watteau picture, alight with laughter and faint scandalous deliciousness.

The Pierrots creep from their hiding-places, up to the back, whence each hopes to have a better view of his adored. So engrossed with his own cautious progress is each that they find themselves tiptoeing straight into the grotesque and alarming form of the Negro servant, who, though small, is a terrifying object to a love-lorn Pierrot. His eyes roll white in his black face ; the intruders disappear hastily behind the trees right and left of the centre back.

Now the Marquise speaks graciously to the girls. ' Play your games of cat's-cradle, my children.' She smiles, and motions the servant to come forward. Obediently, he comes, with fantastic tread, bearing upon a silver tray a length of scarlet ribbon. He bows, presents the ribbon to the first girl, and retires once more to his place. The girls play at cat's-cradle together, while the Marquise watches them graciously. She does not notice that two white faces are watching her, first from behind the trees, and then from behind the Negro servant as he stands immovable, save for the rolling and suspicious eyes.

At last one of the girls tangles the ribbon, and, tired of the game, throws it down and runs, petulantly, out of sight. The other asks the Marquise's permission to follow her. The lady motions her away, and bids the servant begone, too, so that she may be left alone a little with her book.

The Pierrots, in an agony of hope, watch his pompous exit, and each prepares to be left alone with the object of his passion. As usual, they have forgotten each other !

E.   The Marquise sits dreamily upon the seat. Pierrot Noir, with splendid step and gesture, places himself in the best position to call attention to himself and to approach her

'PIERROT CONTENT,' BY WATTEAU

COSTUMES FOR PIERROT BLANC AND MARQUISE IN 'THE PIERROTS AT VERSAILLES'

with suitable dignity. He stands a second up left, prepared to make the first step, when—Pierrot Blanc dashes in front of him with the same intent, and they advance simultaneously, Pierrot Blanc leading. But Pierrot Noir will not bear it. He catches Pierrot Blanc by the shoulder and draws him back to the starting-point, placing himself ostentatiously in front. Once more they advance slowly and simultaneously. By now the Marquise has seen them, and is much intrigued by the curious little manikins that have appeared in her garden so suddenly.

Before Pierrot Noir can speak, his rival has dragged him back once more, and stands centre, saying, ' Madame, *I* have brought these lilies for your acceptance ' ; and he kneels to give his offering. But Pierrot Noir has dashed round to the other side of the seat where *he* is, saying, ' But *I* have brought you this exquisite poem.'

At the same moment they rise, and each taking what he believes to be the centre of the stage, announces, ' I love you.' The last flourish of their splendid gesture brings them face to face. They have spoken, not to the Marquise, but to each other ! Their rage finds vent in a resounding if somewhat childish stamp, which brings them heroically back to back. Tableaux.

The Marquise rises. These charming children must not spoil the beauty of the night by quarrelling in her garden. Besides, they are amusing. She will look at them closer. So she comes round behind them and taps them simultaneously on the shoulders.

They spring apart, each saying to himself, ' Ah, she has noticed me.' She sweeps between them, shaking a cautionary finger, and circles the stage, they following eagerly.

Once more she lingers centre. Each Pierrot says to himself, ' This is my chance.' They prepare ; they speak. ' I love you,' they say, as they fling themselves upon one knee, offering their gifts to the Marquise, who finds them both adorably entertaining. She bends to each and graciously accepts their offerings.

But, heavens, some one is coming ! The Marquise is a little flustered ; the Pierrots arè alarmed. She flies to the seat ; they stand a moment behind it ; and, then, to be sure that no unfair advantages are taken, each extinguishes the other by placing a hand on his head and pushing his rival out of sight behind the back of the seat.

F.   Only just in time. The Negro servant returns, establishes himself centre back with his accustomed fantastic dignity, and announces, ' Monsieur is on his way here.'

The Marquise is amused at the situation in which she finds herself. But the heads of two alarmed Pierrots rise from behind her. ' Hush ! ' she says to them in turn ; and once more they extinguish each other.

The Marquise, with a twinkle of enjoyment in her adorable eyes, takes two red roses from the breast of her gown ; one she slips into the centre of White Pierrot's sheaf of lilies, the other she folds into the scroll of Black Pierrot's poem. Then she sits, exquisitely composed, to await the arrival of Monsieur le Marquis.

He appears, gloriously apparelled, and followed by the two Jeunes Filles, in a twitter of excitement. ' M. le Marquis is so handsome and he is sure to have brought some beautiful offering for Madame la Marquise.' He has. He opens the leather case he carries, lifts from it a priceless necklace of diamonds, and handing the case nonchalantly to the servant, offers the necklace to Madame with a bow of the purest gallantry. With what a grace she accepts it and lays it round her snowy neck for him to admire. But he has yet another gift for her. From his own finger he draws a ring of beautiful workmanship. It sparkles richly as he places it on her hand. Madame is delighted. Such taste, such perfect manners. Now, M. le Marquis offers her the tips of his exquisite fingers and asks her to accept his company within doors. Together, like two expensive puppets moved by invisible strings, they pass away out of sight. The little girls are left to sigh, ' Ah ! what a husband ! ' and to follow at a discreet distance. The servant follows also, with the leisured indolence of one whose work is accomplished, and who is about to join the gentlemen's gentlemen.

The Pierrots are alone once more. Two white, dejected

faces have watched the little scene of the return of the most unsatisfactory wealthy husband of the object of their adoration. As the Marquise passes out of sight, they are left, still kneeling behind the seat, only their heads showing above it, each saying the fatal word, ' Married ! ' Tableaux of despair.

G.   Pierrot Blanc rises dejectedly. He walks slowly and sadly to the centre and up towards the back. Then he turns. He remembers the sheaf of white lilies. He might as well take them with him. She forgot them—hardly noticed them in fact—but they were good lilies and it is a pity to waste them. He returns, slowly picks up the bouquet, and as slowly returns to centre. There his grief overcomes him. He sniffs, his shoulders heave, he sobs in time to the music.

Now Pierrot Noir rises. He catches sight of the poem he wrote for Her. He cannot leave it behind to be scorned, perhaps, or merely overlooked. He picks it up. Then his grief breaks out, and he, too, sobs, by the corner of the seat, in time to the music.

Adversity is a great softener of the temper. The two Pierrots catch sight of each other. Still weeping bitterly, Pierrot Blanc holds out his arms ; Pierrot Noir staggers into them. They sob with great energy in each other's arms, still in time to the music.

H.   When—suddenly—light breaks. Each sees, over the other's shoulder, his own offering, and nestling in the centre of it a deep red rose. Breathless with excitement, and once more oblivious of each other, they draw out the precious emblems. Exultant, they circle the stage until they arrive once more back to back, where they speak again together in the splendid gesture of well-earned triumph, ' She loves *me* ! '

Success can afford to be magnanimous. Rivalry is forgotten. Generous, each in the joy of his own supposed success, they remember one another, and holding the precious roses in their free hands, they embrace fervently. ' Brother,' they say, ' Brother ! '

And the moon laughs on the Pierrots in the Gardens at Versailles.

NOTES ON MUSIC

Music Required :

Nachtstücke. Opus 23	Schumann
Fantasiestücke. Opus 111	Schumann
My Ladye's Minuet	F. Swinstead

(All published by Augener & Co., Ltd.)

A.   *Nachtstücke.* No. 3.   *The Vision of the Marquise*

Repeat first 8 bars. Play to 32nd bar. Cut to end

Curtain music	8 bars
Entrance of Girls	8 bars
Entrance of Marquise—her moves and exit ..	24 bars

B.   *Nachtstücke.* No. 1.   *Entrance of the Pierrots*

Play 32 bars. Cut to end

Entrance of Pierrot Blanc	8 bars
Entrance of Pierrot Noir	8 bars
Both to up left and down right and meet centre ..	8 bars
Run away to corners, see each other, go centre ..	8 bars

C.   *Fantasiestücke.* No. 3.   *Their Quarrel*

Play 16 bars. Cut 32 bars. Play to end (8 bars)

Pierrot Noir : ' You here ? Why ? '	2 bars
Pierrot Blanc : ' You here ? Why ? '	2 bars
Pierrot Noir : ' You go away '	2 bars
Pierrot Blanc : ' I stay here '	2 bars
Both Pierrots : ' We stay here. Why ? '	4 bars
Both Pierrots : ' She walks up and down ' ..	4 bars
Pierrot Noir : ' I have poem '	2 bars
Pierrot Blanc : ' I have flowers '	2 bars
Both Pierrots : ' I adore her '	4 bars

D.   *My Ladye's Minuet.*   *The Marquise and the Girls*

Play 42 bars. Cut 16 bars. Play to end (45 bars)

Introduction. Pierrots to corners	2 bars
Entrance of Servant	8 bars
Entrance of Marquise and Girls. Sit	12 bars
Pierrots up to back	15 bars

Marquise speaks (a) to Girls	5 bars
(b) to Servant	6 bars
Servant to Girls with ribbon	8 bars
First Girl makes cat's-cradle (Pierrots behind Servant)	4 bars
Second Girl takes it	4 bars
First Girl takes it and Second Girl muddles it	8 bars
First Girl up and run off	4 bars
Second Girl up and run off	4 bars
Servant bows and off	7 bars

E. *Nachtstücke.* No. 4.   *The Pierrot's Declaration*

Play straight through

Pierrots to up left—Blanc in front	2 bars
Walk towards Marquise—Blanc in front—and back to corner, changing places	4 bars
Walk towards Marquise—Noir in front. Blanc pulls Noir back and steps in front	4 bars
Blanc speaks. Noir to down left	4 bars
Noir speaks. Both to centre	4 bars
Both : ' I love you.' Meet centre	4 bars
Marquise between them—round left and back to centre. Pierrots following ; finish Blanc down right. Noir down left	11 bars
Both : ' I love you.' Kneel, offering gifts	4 bars
She takes them. Picture. Hush ! She sits. Pierrots behind seat	8 bars

F. *My Ladye's Minuet.*   *Monsieur le Marquis*

Play 42 bars. Cut 16 bars. Play to end (45 bars)

Introduction	2 bars
Entrance of Servant	8 bars
Servant : ' M'sieu from there to here is coming.' Bow	12 bars
Pierrots heads up. Extinguish each other	8 bars
Marquise puts roses in Pierrots' gifts	18 bars
Entrance of Marquis and Girls	8 bars
Marquis speaks and gives necklace	8 bars
Gives ring	8 bars
Says : ' You and I into the house,' and gives hand	4 bars
Exeunt Marquis, Marquise, Servant, Girls to down	

centre and say, ' Married ! " Pierrots up and
say, ' Married ! ' .. .. 11 bars

G. *Nachtstücke.* No. 1. *The Pierrots' Despair*

Play 24 bars. Cut to end

Pierrot Blanc away to centre. Noir, head on arms 8 bars
Pierrot Blanc takes flowers and goes centre .. 4 bars
Pierrot Noir takes poem and goes down right .. 4 bars
Both turn. Noir goes up to centre. Embrace .. 4 bars
Sob .. .. 4 bars

H. *Nachtstücke.* No. 4. *The Pierrots' Joy*

Play 10 bars. Cut to end

Both see flowers. Break away .. .. .. 2 bars
Take out flower. Kiss it .. .. 4 bars
Pierrot Blanc round left and to up centre. Noir to
down right .. .. 2 bars
Both say : ' She loves me ! ' Picture .. .. 2 bars

COSTUME

Period : Eighteenth Century

Pierrot Blanc :

White Pierrot suit, loose trousers and coat, edged with narrow
band of green. Green pom-poms.
White ruff.
White stockings.
White shoes, heeled and buckled.
White skull-cap.
White make-up.

Pierrot Noir :

Black Pierrot suit, trimmed green as above.
Black ruff.
Black stockings.
Black shoes.
Black skull-cap.
White make-up.

Madame la Marquise :

Buckle shoes.
White silk stockings.
Panniers.

Silk or brocade dress, with low, square-cut neck and sleeves to just below the elbow, finished with lace.

Hair : White wig dressed low on the top, or own hair. Small wreath of roses fixed at the side.

Monsieur le Marquis :

Black buckle shoes with red heels.
White silk stockings.
Satin knee-breeches.
Skirted coat, in satin or brocade.
Embroidered waistcoat.
Lace jabot.
Lace ruffles at the wrist.
White or grey powdered wig, the queue tied with black *moiré* ribbon.

Jeunes Filles :

Flat shoes, rose-coloured.
White silk stockings.
Eighteenth-century ballet dresses, with short sleeves, fitting bodices, outlined at neck with flowers, one pale pink, one pale blue.
Full petticoats (tarlatan). Small flower-wreath on the hair, which is smoothly dressed and unpowdered.

Negro Servant :

Baggy red or blue trousers.
Dull gold tunic coat, sleeveless, over yellow shirt. Emerald green waist-binding, with long ends edged with gold fringe.
Red Eastern shoes.
Yellow turban.
Black make-up.

PROPERTY PLOT

Stage :

Rostrum in opening centre back.
3 tread steps.
Ditto off stage up right.
Stone garden seat.
Curtain set, or tree-cloth at back.
Sky cloth, lit night-blue.

Hand :

Book	*Marquis*
Two red roses	*Marquise*
Sheaf of lilies	*Pierrot Blanc*
Scroll of poem	*Pierrot Noir*
Silver tray	*Servant*
Length of narrow scarlet ribbon	*Ditto*
Diamond necklace in case	*Marquis*
Diamond ring	*Ditto*

THE MARRIAGE OF COLUMBINE

(Music selected from works by Leonard Butler and Alec Rowley.)

The play has been performed at The Arts Theatre, London, July 1928, and has formed part of the examination plays performed by students of the Central School of Speech Training and Dramatic Art, London, for the Diploma in Dramatic Art of the University of London. It has also formed part of the programmes of Ginner-Mawer Company performances in Hyde Park, under the auspices of the League of Arts. The play was on all occasions produced by the author.

THE MARRIAGE OF COLUMBINE

*It is the day of Columbine's wedding, and as she is the love
of all the town, all the town is there to see. Columbine is marrying
Scaramouche. ' How fortunate,' sigh all the girl friends. ' How
desperate,' sigh all her rejected suitors. ' How ravishing she
looks,' say all the bridesmaids. ' How exquisitely pretty the
bridesmaids are,' say all the groomsmen. Columbine says
nothing, but the tears still lingering in her pretty eyes speak for
her. Pierrot says, ' I shall die' ; Harlequin says, ' Nonsense, I
shall marry her myself.'*

*The time is Victorian, when weddings were so fine, and
everybody had so many relations. They all came to the wedding,
so the company consists of :*

Columbine	*A Bride*
Her Father	*A Man of Property*
Her Mother	*A Perfect Lady*
Scaramouche..	*A Bridegroom with more Wealth than Beauty.*

Harlequin
Pierrot
Bridesmaids
Groomsmen
Columbine's Girl Friends
. Rejected Suitors
Friends of the Family, and—
    other Relations.

*The scene is laid outside the Church. Up right are steps
leading into the Church.*

A.   The curtain rises on an empty scene ; then there enter
three of Columbine's girl friends, all a-twitter with excitement.
They make a group centre, and chatter together.

First Girl : ' She is to be married ! '

Second Girl : ' And he has money in piles and piles ; like this ! '

Third Girl : ' Oh, but her dress is so exquisite ! '

And they all sigh in ecstasy at the remembrance of a glimpse of Columbine dressed for her wedding. And there are other things—frilly, lacy things—only to be mentioned in whispers ; and three little heads are placed close together, inside three large bonnets, while three small pairs of feet can hardly keep still below three frilly crinolines.

But the sounds of the wedding cortège are heard approaching, and the girls break away, up stage right, determined to have the best view of everything.

B.   The sounds of the wedding procession draw nearer. And there enter the lady and gentlemen friends of the family in couples and little groups, preceded by the first lady and gentlemen, who move to the centre, discussing their own clothes and other people's. The men, conscious of extra high collars, flowered waistcoats just a shade tighter than is comfortable, of high hats a little too small in the head, carnations in buttonholes, and yellow gloves with elusive buttons ; the ladies conscious of their own toilet well performed, but suspicious of each other's billowing perfections. Every one is a little strained, but expectant.

The first lady speaks to her husband : ' She is to be married.'

He replies : ' The fellow has money, I hear. Quite satisfactory.'

Two of Columbine's rejected lovers have joined the crowd. There is despair in their whiskers and high black hats, despair in their very boots and gloves.

First Suitor : ' She is to be married ! '

Second Suitor : 'He is fat ! '

Both : ' We are very depressed. Ah ! How exquisite she is ! '

Now, from down right and left come the immortal lovers of Columbine, Harlequin and Pierrot. In spite of the very Victorian costumes of the other guests they keep their

GIRL FRIENDS OF THE BRIDE
IN 'THE MARRIAGE OF COLUMBINE'
From 'Modes de Paris,' 1838

traditional clothes; Harlequin, the eternally successful lover, long, slim and graceful, always smiling behind his black half-mask, always half dancing with his long spangled legs, a red rose pinned to his sweeping black cloak, and his wand at his side to show he is still Mercury, the Messenger of the Gods. He has a coil of rope over one arm.

Pierrot is the poet-lover, always a-dream when action is required, with his white face matching his white suit, and his long, white hands a-droop, or feeling for his poem or his pen. They meet down centre, back to back, but, being absorbed each in his own reflections, do not notice each other.

Pierrot, very depressed : ' She is to be married ! I shall die at her feet ! '

Harlequin : ' Personally, I shall marry her myself.'

They are lost in the crowd, which bustles about the stage, exchanging gossip, and every one hoping to find the best position from which to see the arrival of the bride.

At last she comes, all veiled and rather downcast, leaning on her father's arm. She might be any little Victorian bride, followed by her bridesmaids, with their stiff posies of flowers, but *we* know that she is Columbine, because her little wings are showing between her shoulders, and we feel that at any moment she might fly away once more to Mount Olympus. Her mother follows with her handkerchief held to her eyes in a very genteel manner.

Alone, and in splendid raiment, which includes a large cloak and plumed hat that he must have brought from Italy long years ago, comes Scaramouche. He looks like an ordinary man of wealth, if a little odd in dress, save that the size of his nose and stomach are strangely reminiscent of masks and carnivals. He is followed by the groomsmen, immaculate young gentlemen with peg-top trousers and side-whiskers.

When all the company is collected, Columbine's father pompously announces that his daughter is about to wed Scaramouche. He joins their hands, and bids the guests proceed into the church. They do so, rustling expensively and saying once more : ' The sweet child. Such a good match ' ; ' I hardly care for green feathers myself,' etc., etc.

Scaramouche precedes them, a very affable bridegroom—
not young perhaps, but his watch-chain testifies to his highly
satisfactory bank balance.

· Columbine's mother and father turn up stage, chatting
with their guests, and linger a moment at the foot of the
steps, back to audience, to wrestle with a particularly evasive
button of father's right glove. The bridesmaids kneel behind
the bride, adjusting the flowers on the train of her dress.
Columbine, very agitated behind her veil, remains practically
alone for a moment with her two lovers, Harlequin and
Pierrot.

C.   Pierrot approaches her very diffidently and sorrowfully,
and says : ' Do lift your veil.'

Timidly she raises it, and looks at him. At the sight of
her dear little tear-stained face Pierrot falls on his knees,
and kisses the hem of her dress. What else can he do, he is
so poor ? But he offers her his last poem, ' Ode to an Angel
being Married.' She kisses it and hides it in her dress, almost
crying for the sorrow of poor gentle Pierrot, who has loved
her so faithfully. Pierrot turns away. She is lost to him.

D.   Then Harlequin, still gallant and smiling, approaches from
the other side. She daren't look at him. He does make her
heart flutter so. But somehow one of her hands is in his,
and—and—he is kissing it. And :

' Columbine,' he says, ' I love you.'

Her heart flutters so terribly. What *is* to be done ? She
never can resist him when he talks like that. Her hands try
to still the little beating heart. She knows she will look at
him in a moment. She had better swoon.

She swoons, into the arms of the bewildered and tearful
bridesmaids.

Pierrot is aghast. Harlequin turns away with a strangely
confident smile—perhaps he had seen a lady swoon before.
Columbine's father and mother turn, horrified to find their
child unconscious, almost at the altar-steps. Father fumes,
and, extracting, with considerable difficulty, a large bandana
handkerchief from a pocket in the tails of his coat, fans

Columbine's face, purple himself with anxiety, heat, rage, and unaccustomedly tight garments. Mother takes Columbine's limp hand and pats it agitatedly, wishing she had brought the smelling-salts.

Harlequin approaches Father as the latter turns away hopelessly from his child, who, as usual, is upsetting all his plans at the last moment.

Harlequin : ' Sir, will you permit me ? I think I have a remedy.'

Father : ' Oh ! Anything you like, my dear fellow. I wash my hands of these d—— women, and their swoonings and what-nots.'

Harlequin takes the rose from his cloak, and, slipping into it a note he has prepared, places the rose beneath Columbine's nose. Her mother is now weeping into her handkerchief, and so does not notice that her daughter opens her eyes suspiciously suddenly at that well-known scent. Harlequin whispers : ' Hush,' and points to the concealed note. Columbine looks at it. Smiles, and nods, ' I understand.' Then she slowly and deliberately rises to her feet, the perfectly composed little bride. Perhaps the bridesmaids saw, but Harlequin is such a dear, and their darling Columbine is smiling serenely once more. So who cares ? Not they, the little minxes.

E.   Now father pulls out his watch. They are gerting late as usual. Columbine has recovered ? Thank heaven for that. These women—well—well. Columbine passes into church with her bridesmaids and her parents. But on the top step she manages to turn and give Harlequin a little wave of the hand, and Harlequin, now in the centre of the stage, throws a thousand kisses after the demurest little bride who ever wore orange-blossom.

When Columbine looks like that, and Harlequin starts throwing kisses, you may be sure something is going to happen.

F.   Of course Harlequin has a plan. He calls to Pierrot, who joins him. ' These cords,' he says, ' are to bind the old man in there.'

' Oh,' says Pierrot, mystified but hopeful.

' But first,' says Harlequin, ' he must be brought out here.'

' Oh,' says Pierrot again.

' I have it,' says Harlequin, ' you take this note to him.'

' I see,' says Pierrot, light dawning on his rather slow intelligence.

Harlequin takes him by the shoulders, and, like conspirators, they approach the church door, and Harlequin pushes him in. While he is alone, Harlequin hides beside the church door, and gets ready his bat. Scaramouche comes out, pompously, to inquire who dares to send for him at the very moment when he is about to be married. Harlequin leaps upon him from behind, fells him with his bat, and gags him. But first he has whipped off his cloak and hat. Now Pierrot brings the cords and helps to bind Scaramouche. Before the astonished little fat man has realized what has happened, they have rolled him away into a corner, left, and Harlequin orders Pierrot to sit on his chest. This he does with relish, and at once begins to write a triumphant ' Ode on the Defeat of an Enemy.' While he is so engaged, Harlequin whips a false nose from his pocket, puts on Scaramouche's hat and cloak, and departs pompously into the church to take the place of the now prostrate bridegroom. Pierrot realizes the full meaning of the plot too late, but rushes in after him.

G.   Gagged and bound Scaramouche lies, near to explosion with rage and injured dignity, while, from the church, come sounds of the Marriage Service in progress. Scaramouche struggles to a sitting position, but as the Wedding March is heard, he falls back, purple in the face.

H.   Now the church doors open, and the guests, bridesmaids, and groomsmen pour out, chattering about the brilliant event, all anxious to see the happy pair come out of church. When, crash ! Before their horrified gaze there rolls a dishevelled form. Can this be Scaramouche, the wealthy, the affable bridegroom ? It is. . . . Panic ensues.

THE BRIDE'S MOTHER
IN 'THE MARRIAGE OF COLUMBINE'
From 'Modes de Paris,' 1838

I. The bridesmaids faint into the arms of the groomsmen. The little minxes, as if they hadn't known all the time ! The ladies rush forward, and bend over the still-writhing Scaramouche. They fling their hands to heaven and retreat hastily. Such language ! The men advance towards him, but the ladies call them back, and everybody moves in an agitated circle round the still prostrate form ; of course nobody *does* anything. Father and mother appear on the church steps. The crowd gives way and points to what lies on the ground. ' Here is the bridegroom ! '

Father advances, and says, ' Untie him, some one,' and a good deal more as well. Mother weeps. The crowd is distraught, as a fuming Scaramouche, free at last, staggers to his feet, demanding immediate satisfaction from some one. And, upon the top of the steps appear, smiling, radiant, a very newly married Columbine and her bridegroom, Harlequin.

J. Amid the general consternation the newly wedded lovers humbly approach Columbine's father and beg for his forgiveness. It is easy to be humble when the game is won. They have no arguments in their favour, save their youth.

Father is not impressed. He is, indeed, very angry, and not at all sure that he has not been made a fool of ; uncertain whether she is pleased or distressed, mother once more takes refuge in genteel tears.

But Scaramouche, thirsting for revenge of some kind, catches sight of Pierrot. ' Ah, it was he who brought the false message. He is the root of all the trouble.'

Scaramouche makes for the unfortunate Pierrot, who, though sad that he yet again has lost his Columbine, is, for once, quick enough, and dodges away among the crowd and out of sight, down right, Scaramouche panting after him.

Harlequin and Columbine together make the ever-simple, indisputable remarks, ' I love him ' and ' I love her.'

With the departure of the enraged ex-bridegroom a gloom is lifted from the assembly. After all, Harlequin is obviously so much better suited to Columbine than the unattractive Scaramouche.

Father realizes that nothing can be done, and so decides to be magnanimous. ' Let us avoid a scandal at all costs.' He lays his hands in blessing upon the two culprits still kneeling before him.

Harlequin raises his blushing little bride. He kisses her before them all. Who could resist kissing Columbine as a bride ?

K. The wedding procession forms once more, and, amid showers of rose-leaves and confetti, Harlequin leads Columbine away to the wedding breakfast.

As the last guests are disappearing, Pierrot, still running, rushes across the front of the stage, pursued by a panting Scaramouche. As usual Pierrot is the scapegoat for Harlequin's pranks. But Columbine still carries his poem near her happy little heart.

NOTES ON MUSIC

Music required :

Village Reminiscences	Leonard Butler
(Published by Augener & Co., Ltd.)	
Valentines	Leonard Butler
(Published by Lengnick.)	
An Ayre and March	Jeremiah Clarke
	(arr. by Alec Rowley)
(Published by Winthrop Rogers.)	

A. *Village Reminiscences :* ' High in the Belfry ' .. Butler

    Entrance of Columbine and Girl Friends

Introduction	8 bars
Entrance of girls	8 bars
First girl : ' She is to marry him '	8 bars
Second girl : ' He has money in piles and piles ' ..	8 bars
Third girl : ' Her dress and veil are exquisite ' ..	8 bars
All run to centre	8 bars
They lead round into a diagonal line right ..	8 bars

B. *March.* .. .. Clarke

    Entrance of Friends, Bridal Procession, Pierrot and Harlequin

Introduction	8 bars

Entrance of ladies and gentlemen. First couple
    move to centre ..   ..   4 bars
First lady : ' She is to be married '   ..   ..   4 bars
First gentlemen : ' He has plenty of money '   ..   4 bars
Entrance of rejected suitors ..   ..   4 bars
They say : ' She is to be married.' ' He is fat.'
    ' I shall die.'   ..   ..   8 bars
General movement ..   ..   12 bars
Entrance of Harlequin and Pierrot   ..   ..   4 bars
Pierrot : ' She is to be married. I shall die.'   ..   4 bars
Harlequin : ' I shall marry her myself.' ..   ..   4 bars
Entrance of bride, her father and mother, brides-
    maids and bridegroom ..   ..   8 bars
Father joins the hands of Scaramouche and
    Columbine   ..   ..   4 bars
The guests, followed by Scaramouche, go into
    church   ..   ..   11 bars

C.   *Valentines.* No. 1.   ..   ..   Butler

Play 17 bars

Pierrot and Columbine

Pierrot crosses to Columbine   ..   ..   ..   5 bars
Pierrot : ' You lift your veil.' She does so ; he
    kneels   ..   ..   4 bars
He kisses her dress and gives her a poem   ..   4 bars
She looks at it and puts it in her dress   ..   ..   4 bars

D.   *Valentines.* No. 7.   ..   ..   Butler

Harlequin and Columbine

Harlequin crosses to Columbine   ..   ..   ..   5 bars
He kisses her hand and says : ' I love you.'   ..   8 bars
Columbine faints   ..   ..   4 bars
Father and mother come down to Columbine   ..   8 bars
Father fans her with his handkerchief. Mother
    pats her hand   ..   ..   8 bars
Harlequin goes to father   ..   ..   5 bars
Harlequin : ' Can I do anything ? ' Father : ' Yes,
    do, do ! ' ..   ..   4 bars
Harlequin goes to Columbine and gives her the
    rose. She opens her eyes   ..   ..   ..   4 bars
Harlequin says : ' Hush ! ' Columbine reads the
    note, stands up and all hold the picture   ..   8 bars

E. *March.* .. .. **Clarke**

Last 11 bars only

Columbine and Bridesmaids into Church

F. *Village Reminiscences.* Madrigal. .. .. .. **Butler**

The Plot

Harlequin fetches cords	4 bars
Harlequin calls Pierrot to centre	4 bars
Harlequin says : ' These cords to bind him, but first he must come here '	8 bars
Harlequin gives note to Pierrot and both turn ..	9 bars
Pierrot and Harlequin move up to steps ; Pierrot exits	4 bars

On Repeat :

Harlequin prepares rope, hat and gag, and goes up right centre	8 bars
Enter Scaramouche ; Harlequin strikes him ..	4 bars
They bind Scaramouche	4 bars
Roll him to left	4 bars
Pierrot sits on him. Harlequin puts on cloak and hat	5 bars
Harlequin exit into church followed by Pierrot ..	4 bars

G. *Wedding March.* .. .. **Mendelssohn**

Play 8 bars

Scaramouche struggles to sitting position and falls back

H. *March.* .. .. **Clarke**

First 20 bars followed by roll in bass

Guests out of Church

On roll Scaramouche rolls into centre

I. *Village Reminiscences.* ' The Carrier's Song ' .. **Butler**

General Consternation of Guests

Ladies into centre and out	4 bars
Men into centre and out	4 bars
All round in circle to left	4 bars
All round in circle to right	4 bars
Father and mother appear on steps ; move down. Father says : ' Untie him '	4 bars

THE GUESTS
IN 'THE MARRIAGE OF COLUMBINE
From 'Modes de Paris,' 1838

Scaramouche up	4 bars
Harlequin and Columbine appear on steps	4 bars

J. *Ayre.* .. .. Clarke

Columbine and Harlequin pray for Forgiveness

Harlequin and Columbine to father	4 bars
They kneel	4 bars
Scaramouche sees Pierrot and chases him off	4 bars
Harlequin and Columbine speak together ..	2 bars
Father blesses them ; they get up ..	6 bars
They come down centre and turn towards exit ..	5 bars

K. *March.* .. .. Clarke

Last 23 bars only

Exit Harlequin and Columbine followed by father, mother and crowd	16 bars
Scaramouche chases Pierrot across the front ..	7 bars

COSTUME

Period : 1838

Columbine :

Wedding dress in white muslin or organdie, with fitting
bodice, off the shoulders.

Short sleeves, frilled, to elbow.

Orange blossom.

Large crinoline hoop.

Veil with wreath of orange blossom.

White three-quarter-length gloves.

Small circular bouquet.

White stockings.

Flat black sandal shoes.

Bridesmaids :

Dresses in muslin or organdie, white with dotted or lined
pattern.

Fitting bodices, off the shoulders, with short sleeves, frilled,
to the elbow.

Flounced skirts to the ground.

Large crinoline hoops.

Sandal shoes.

White stockings.

Three-quarter-length gloves.

Bouquets.

Hair : In knot or rolls at the back, with curls hanging on each side of the face.

Spray or wreath of roses.

Columbine's Mother :

Purple or green shot silk gown over large crinoline. Fitting bodice with long sleeves.

Green dolman, or embroidered shawl.

Poke bonnet (well back on the head) in lavender silk, with curtain veil at the back ; sprays of flowers on and inside the brim.

Fawn or coloured gloves.

White stockings.

Black sandal shoes.

Girl Friends :

Crinoline dresses in silk or muslin, in pale shades. Fitting bodices with low necks, elbow sleeves.

Poke bonnets.

Shawls optional.

Lady Guests :

As illustration, or other dresses of the period, with bonnets and shawls.

(For all above costumes see illustrations.)

Harlequin :

Spangled Harlequin suit.

Black skull-cap.

Ruffle.

Cloak.

White stockings.

Sandal shoes.

Harlequin bat.

Pierrot :

White Pierrot suit, with loose coat, trousers, ruffle.

Black or white skull-cap.

White shoes and stockings.

Bride's Father, Rejected Suitors, Groomsmen :
Men's costumes for 1838.
Tight-fitting trousers in buff or grey, strapped under patent-leather boots or shoes.
Flowered satin double-breasted waistcoats.
Tail coats in brown or dark blue.
Stock collars with broad ties.
Lavender or yellow gloves.
Top-hats.
Side whiskers.
Wigs.

Scaramouche :
As above, with large black cloak and wide-brimmed black felt hat.
Gold fob or watch-chain.
Rings.

PROPERTY PLOT

Stage :
Rostrum.
3 tread steps.
Dark backing behind rostrum.
Steps leading off rostrum, off stage.
Curtain set.

Hand :

Coil of rope	*Harlequin*
Rose	*Ditto*
2 pieces of paper	*Harlequin*
Quill pen and 2 pieces of paper..	*Pierrot*
Watch	*Father*
Bandana Handkerchief	*Ditto*
Handkerchief .. .. ··	*Mother*
Gag	*Harlequin*

PIERROT'S GARDEN

(Music selected from ' L'Almanach aux Images '
by Gabrièl Grovlez.)

The play has been performed at the Albert Hall Theatre, forming part of a lecture-demonstration to the Summer School of the Central School of Speech Training and Dramatic Art, 1931.

CAST :

Pierrot	..	.. ..	*Joyce Ruscoe.*
His Wife	..	.. ..	*Irene Mawer.*

Produced by the author.

PIERROT'S GARDEN

Pierrot has a garden. That is partly because he is married, and partly because he likes flowers. If you are married you need to feel a Man of Property, and if you love Columbine, you are almost sure to like flowers, because she does. So Pierrot has a garden ; it is not a large garden, it consists of a pleasant green tub full of earth ; at present, it contains nothing else, but this play is concerned with the remedying of that. As Pierrot is a gardener, of course he also owns a trowel and a watering-can. He is newly married, and consequently rather excited and important, and the persons of the play are just simply

Pierrot and
His Wife, who was Columbine, but who has now
    settled, she hopes, into domesticity.

The Scene is an open space outside Pierrot's house. Down right stands the pleasant green tub of earth, with a stick in it to help to train the flowers when they begin to grow, while, up right, are arranged, neatly, Pierrot's trowel and watering-can.

It is a bright and sunny morning, the birds are busy, and it's just the sort of weather that makes even the most lugubrious gardener say, ' Grand growin' weather ! '

A.   Pierrot evidently feels the same. For he enters with jaunty step from up left, carrying, with great care, in the palm of his left hand, a large, important-looking seed. He holds up the seed in his right hand so that we can see it, then puts it back and says, ' I shall plant my seed, and then it will grow into a great big flowering-tree.' Enchanted with the idea, he lays the seed carefully on the ground, walks with deliciously important and excited steps up right, and returns with his trowel. He kneels beside the tub and prepares to dig a hole, when . . . !

Horror ! He sees a large and wriggling worm ! But dangers must be faced—no real gardener is afraid of a worm.

So very cautiously he picks it up between finger and thumb. It wriggles horribly, and he nearly drops it, when, from a tree on his left, a bird chirps suddenly and hungrily. Much relieved to be rid of the responsibility, Pierrot throws away the worm and tells the bird to come and fetch it.

Now he returns to the important business of digging a hole for his seed. This done, he picks up the seed, places it carefully in the hole, pats down the earth over it—and sits back on his heels to await events. He is rather hazy as to how long a seed will take to grow, as he is new to gardening, but he supposes it cannot be long before the first shoot appears. He is doomed to disappointment; nothing happens at all. Gardening is dull work.

Then suddenly a bright idea occurs to him. One waters things when they are first planted, of course; how foolish of him to forget.

Happily excited by his great idea, Pierrot trots up right once more and returns with his watering-can.

He waters the seed, puts down the can, and again watches anxiously. But—nothing appears. He stands sulkily beside his empty garden, the disappointed artist.

B. Now his wife appears from the house. She never can stay indoors doing the housework when the sun is shining. She looks cautiously to see if Pierrot is there, and then, all Columbine, and very little married woman, she flies towards him, only to be greeted with a most unpromising-looking back. 'Dear, dear, dear, *now* what's upset him ? ' she wonders, and, once more the helpful little wife, she approaches him, taps him on the shoulder and says, ' What is the matter, my dear ? '

Pierrot turns to her, points tragically to the seed, and says, ' Damn thing won't *grow* ! '

' Oh, poor Pierrot,' says the little wife, patting his head, consolingly. As she does so, she notices a spray of roses tucked into her dress, and she has her Great Idea.

She leads Pierrot up to the back and tells him to hide his eyes, turning him round with his back to the tub as she does so. He obediently covers his eyes with his hands.

Columbine flies down to the tub, takes the roses from her dress, and fixes them on to the stick which is in the tub, smiling a half-motherly smile as she does so. ' They are easy to manage, these men-children ! ' Then she floats back to Pierrot, turns him round so that he is facing the tub, takes his hands away from his eyes, and standing on tiptoe behind him, blindfolds him with her own.

Together they walk down towards the tub, he blinded and she pushing him. They arrive. She takes away her hands and says, ' Look there ! ' And, behold, his seed has grown (as he always knew it would) into a beautiful little rose-tree with red roses on it. He is not exactly proud. Gardens are like that, if you only know just how to do it.

He must show it to Columbine properly. No mere just running into a thing ; a new rose-tree must be approached with suitable solemnity.

C.   Pierrot springs back to the entrance, offers his arm to Columbine, suggesting that they shall take a stroll round the garden. She is beside him in a moment, her arm in his, the dutiful little wife prepared to admire her lord's domain.

They circle the stage. Pierrot points out the best bits as they pass. Here is the herbaceous border, there are the fruit-trees. She nods, and is duly impressed—they have played the game before.

Then, taken quite by surprise, they arrive at the rose-garden. Pierrot draws her attention to the beautifully-flowering rose-bush. ' A mere trifle, of course, but my own planting.'

Columbine is enchanted. 'How delicious the flowers must smell. Clever Pierrot to grow such a splendid rose-garden ! '

Pierrot's heart stirs. How he loves Columbine—everything he has is hers. He will even pick his rose for her. And splendidly he does so.

Gallantly, he kneels before her, just as he used to do when they were courting. He holds out his precious rose to her, and bends his head for the touch of her hands upon it in blessing.

Perhaps it was lucky that he bent his head just at that

moment. Otherwise even a man could hardly have failed to see that the look she gave him, as she replaced the flowers in her dress in the exact spot from which she had taken them a few moments before, was more motherly than wifely. What she *said* to him was, ' Oh, Pierrot, how good of you to give me your beautiful rose that you grew yourself.' But what she *thought* was, ' Oh, I'm so glad he's never grown up.'

They look very happy in Pierrot's garden as the curtains close upon them.

NOTES ON MUSIC

Music Required :

L'Almanach aux Images	.. ..	Gabriel **Grovlez**

(Published by Augener & Co., Ltd.)

A. *Les Ânes.*   *Pierrot Plants His Seed*

Introduction	4 bars
Enter Pierrot to centre. Holds up and puts back seed	10 bars
' I plant the seed—it grows into big tree ' ..	8 bars
Puts down seed	4 bars
Up and fetch trowel ; back to centre and kneel ..	8 bars
Sees worm ; picks up ; throws away to bird ..	10 bars
Digs	9 bars
Plants seed	4 bars
Pats soil	4 bars
Watches seed ; disappointment	16 bars
Fetches watering-can..	8 bars
Waters ; looks, and nothing happens	5 bars

B. *Chanson de l'Escarpolette.*   *Columbine joins Him*

Enter Columbine to Pierrot ; tap on shoulder ..	16 bars
Pierrot speaks : ' It won't grow '	3 bars
Columbine : ' Oh, poor Pierrot '	6 bars
Idea. Pierrot up stage. Tells him to hide eyes	14 bars
Columbine to tub ; puts flowers in	7 bars
Back to Pierrot ; puts her hands over eyes ..	8 bars
Back to tub ; uncovers eyes ; Pierrot sees flowers	10 bars

C. *Les Ânes.*   *Pierrot Picks the Roses*

Last 32 bars

Both to entrance up left	3 bars
Walk round and to flower-pot	8 bars
Shows flower	8 bars
Pierrot picks flower, kneels and gives it	8 bars
She takes it. Picture	5 bars

PROPERTY PLOT

Curtain or garden set.

Stage :

Wooden tub full of earth, down right.

Trowel $\left.\right\}$ up right
Watering-can

Hand :

Large seed	*Pierrot*
Spray of red roses	*Columbine*

COSTUME

Pierrot :

Black or white Pierrot suit.
Skull-cap.
Ruffle.
Shoes (flat).
Stockings to match suit.
White make-up.

Columbine :

Full dress to ankles ; fitting bodice ; puff sleeves.
Crinoline.
White stockings.
Scarlet unblocked ballet shoes.
Hair : Dressed high at back, parted centre, side curls, bound
with ribbon to match dress.

PRISCILLA, OR THE LOST COLUMBINE

(Music selected from the works of F. Rung, Jean Morel, Alex Roloff, and Moszkowski.)

This play was performed at the Scala Theatre, 1927, when the cast was as follows :

Priscilla	*Irene Mawer*
George, Her Husband	*John Laurie*
First Aunt	*Oonah Todd Naylor*
Second Aunt	*Doris Pillitz*
Clown	*Gwynneth Thurburn*
Pantaloon	*Dilys Harker*
Pierrot	*E. M. Thomas*
Harlequin	*Nina Silcock*

The play has also formed part of the Dramatic Examination performances of the Ginner-Mawer School, and of the Central School of Speech Training and Dramatic Art, for the Diploma in Dramatic Art, of the University of London.

It was, in each case, produced by the author.

PRISCILLA, OR THE LOST COLUMBINE

Once, hundreds of years ago, Columbine lived on Mount Olympus, but her name was Psyche then, and, like all the Dwellers on the Mountain, she was immortal. She wasn't called Columbine until she was travelling through Italy as a serving-maid in the Middle Ages. There she picked up her old friend Hermes,

TRADITIONAL COSTUMES OF CLOWN AND PANTALOON
SHOWING MAKE-UP IN 'PRISCILLA, OR THE LOST COLUMBINE'
(From 'Punch', 1855)

who became her lover Harlequin, living in Bergamo. And there she met Peppe Nappa and Piero, and of course they fell in love with her too, and then she also met Old Pantaleone. She met them all again later in France, where Pierrot spelled his name like that, and became a dreamer and a poet and loved Columbine more than ever, and so did Harlequin. Then they came to England, and Columbine was a dancing-girl. And there they all met their dear friend Joey the clown. And there, as this story tells, a very sad thing happened : Columbine got lost. It was her own fault, because she made a great mistake. But that didn't help matters. Her great mistake was that she got married, a dangerous thing for Columbine to do in any case, but in this case she married the wrong man. At least so her friends said. But she wasn't quite sure about it herself. George, her husband, was certainly ' very Victorian,' and, what was worse, he had two completely Victorian aunts who lived with him even after he was married. And they didn't approve of Columbine (who was called Priscilla), because she couldn't leave off wanting to dance and would wear red ballet-shoes at all hours of the day.

Her friends were very distressed. They had never so completely lost Columbine before, and they determined to get her back again. So Clown and Pantaloon took service with George as butler and footman, and waited their opportunity to bring about a meeting between Priscilla and her old lovers, Pierrot and Harlequin, who meant to try and steal her back again to the Immortals, if only they could get at her, so the characters in the play are :

Priscilla .. *The Lost Columbine, now a prim little Victorian wife, whose feet* will *keep dancing*

George .. *Her husband, who is something successful in the City*

Two very Victorian Aunts

Clown .. ⎰*Now Butler and Footman in Priscilla's*
Pantaloon ⎱ *Home*

Harlequin

Pierrot

It is the day of Priscilla's birthday, and her friends have determined to make the attempt after supper of this day, when, most of all, little wives want to dance and to remember their immortal lovers. The scene is the dining-room of George's house in Bayswater. The table is set half-way up right, with four chairs beside it, one at each end, and two on the up stage side. There is a sideboard against the back wall, left of the centre entrance. The fireplace is down left, and placed diagonally before it is a sofa. The door of the room is up left. But there must be an invisible entrance in the curtains, centre, backed by a sky-cloth lit just like that moonlight night blue that always makes it so difficult for us to resist our dreams. It is evening. Just before dinner-time. The room is lit brightly, but the fire also gives a warm red glow from down left.

A. As the curtain rises the room is empty. But at once there enters, from up left, the First Aunt. She sails in her crinoline to up centre, and is joined there by her sister, the Second Aunt. Together they sail to the sofa by the fire, and at the same moment sit upon it. Still moving simultaneously, they produce two bags, and from them two mufflers and two sets of knitting-needles, which for a moment they click industriously. Then the First Aunt puts down her knitting, calls her sister's attention to the fact that she is about to speak, and speaks.

First Aunt : ' That child has been dancing again.'

Second Aunt : ' Yes, my dear, and showing her ankles.'

Both (with uplifted hands of horror) : ' Disgraceful ! '

B. At this moment Priscilla runs in, her little red shoes twinkling, her eyes alight, her arms full of flowers, and even her prim lavender silk crinoline half suggestive of a remembrance of Columbine, with its little white apron and cherry-coloured bows. Her arms are full of flowers, because it's her birthday, and, mysteriously, these flowers have been left at the door for her. She can't guess by whom, and if Clown and Pantaloon know, they are silent. She runs joyously to down stage centre, and for one moment we are allowed a glimpse of the soul of Columbine inside her, and then, a moment later, she is Priscilla, remembering to make her bobbing curtsies to her husband's aunts.

But her attention is soon distracted from their disapproving glances by the arrival of Clown and Pantaloon with the first necessities for laying the supper. They have a queer, rolling, tumbling gait for a butler and footman. Pantaloon is so bandy-legged, and Clown can hardly restrain himself from turning a somersault every moment. They run queerly across to the table, and begin to lay the cloth as if it were one of the best jokes in the world, and Priscilla joins them, placing her flowers on the table for decoration. She chooses a particularly sweet-smelling rose and lays it in George's place. He is a kind old thing, and she has always wanted him to love her, and it's her birthday, so she does want him to be good-tempered to-night ; but, oh dear ! you never know what sort of a day he may have had in the City, and it does make such a difference to his temper !

All her joyousness of soul is bubbling up inside her. She positively *must* kiss somebody, now this minute. And so, regardless of consequences, she runs across to the sofa, flings her arms round the neck of the astonished First Aunt, and, to that lady's horror, kisses her resoundingly. Will the child never learn manners !

But Priscilla, child indeed that she is, hears a little tune echoing in her head. She dreams a moment of dances she seemed to know in some other life. Then she floatingly dances a few steps down right, turns, and sees Clown. That worthy and Pantaloon have been watching her eagerly. The more Priscilla dances, the better their chance of recapturing Columbine. Clown now opens his arms in a ridiculous invitation, and Priscilla, flying into them, is whirled into an absurd waltz, until, whisking round a corner, the couple crash into the sofa, nearly upsetting the completely scandalized aunts.

Priscilla retreats hastily to the centre. ' Now there will be trouble,' she thinks. Clown is back beside Pantaloon, the perfect footman in a moment, standing stiffly to attention.

The aunts rise to their feet, pictures of outraged propriety. In no uncertain gesture they speak to Priscilla.

First Aunt : ' You are to dance no more.'

Second Aunt : ' And you are *not* to show your ankles.'

Priscilla is penitent. She is always trying to be good, but somehow her feet and her dreams *do* run away with her so. She stands a moment, half tearful. But then, like a grave child repeating a lesson she says : ' I am to dance no more.' And she nods her head firmly several times, as if really trying to remember. But all the same she can't help giving a little flick to her crinoline as she runs back to the table to see if all is ready. And then she hears the sound of George's latch-key.

' George,' say the aunts, ' he must hear of this.'

'The Master,' say Clown and Pantaloon, 'he *will* hear of this.'

'George,' says Priscilla, all in a flutter, ' I do hope he won't hear of this, because I do want him to have remembered my birthday.'

They say all that at once, and there's very little time for them to do more than think it, for now Priscilla is down stage right, smoothing her hair, as George always likes it tidy, and wondering if he will remember to kiss her.

C.   George enters to up centre. Priscilla, looking at him anxiously, fears it has *not* been a good day in the City. There is something forbidding about the side-whiskers protruding from his florid cheeks, and the very angle of the solid gold watch-chain upon his ample waistcoat portends trouble. However, she still hopes . . . It *is* her birthday, and she did look pretty when she peeped in the glass.

But George has handed his hat and stick to Clown and Pantaloon. He moves ponderously down centre, and laying a hand upon the upper region of his waistcoat bows cere-moniously to his aunts. Priscilla is all a-flutter, and looking so kissable—will he ? George looks at her, but does not move beyond the centre, where, advancing a somewhat forbidding whisker, he signifies, ' You may kiss me, Priscilla.' Very damped, poor little Priscilla walks solemnly up to him, lays her fingers on the back of his shoulders to steady herself, rises on tiptoe, and can just reach to plant a disappointed peck on his cheek. She retires again to her corner right, fearing trouble. And here it comes. For the aunts rise simultaneously.

'George,' says the First Aunt, ' listen to me.'

And, ' George,' says the Second Aunt, ' listen to me too.'

George prepares, testily, to listen.

First Aunt : ' That wife of yours has been dancing again.'

Second Aunt : ' And showing her ankles.'

Both : ' It really is disgraceful.'

George turns to the trembling Priscilla, who is already perilously near tears. She *knew* they'd spoil her birthday-party.

'Priscilla,' says George, in his hearthrug manner, 'Have you been dancing?'

'Yes,' nods Priscilla, very quickly, a great many times, so that she shan't burst into tears.

'Well,' says George, as one who speaks for the last time, 'you are to dance *no more.*' And he turns away up left and folds his hands behind his back with complete finality.

Priscilla runs up to him beseechingly. He can't really mean it. But his immovable back, upon which might rest the whole of the British Constitution, is so relentless that she stamps a furious foot at it, and flounces away again, down left, not only near tears this time, but really crying.

D.　But now Clown and Pantaloon appear once more to save the situation. Still ridiculously waddling and dancing, they carry in the rest of the supper, with the dishes held high above their heads, because it's so much more fun to carry things like that than soberly in front of you. They lay the dishes on the table, advance to up stage centre, and with absurd gestures, made simultaneously, say, 'Ladies and gentlemen, the supper is served.'

E.　Priscilla pulls herself together, like the gallant little thing she is. Her supper-party shall be a success after all, with dear Clown and Pantaloon to help her. She runs across to the aunts, and, standing between them, takes a hand of each, and trips across the stage between them as they sail, galleon-wise, to the table. Then she looks at George, and sighs. It would have been fun if he'd offered her his arm, just this once, as it's her birthday, but he's still looking broody! So she runs to him, and placing his hand in the middle of his chest for him, slips her hand into his arm, leads him to his place at the table, and seats herself beside him.

She watches him anxiously. Will he notice the flower she put there for him? He *does* notice it, but, with a gesture of annoyance, throws it away as he unfolds his napkin. 'Really these servants are too careless, leaving things lying about like that!'

Priscilla sighs. George really *isn't* very satisfactory as a lover. But perhaps she was wrong to expect it of a husband. But, somehow or other, she seemed to remember being *tremendously* loved once. But, like her dancing, this memory *can't* be quite nice, the aunts certainly wouldn't approve.

F.   George carves the rabbit pie rather ponderously. Priscilla always has rabbit pie on her birthday, and when they ask her why, she can only say, ' Joey always liked it so,' which never seems sense to anybody but Clown and Pantaloon. These worthies now hand the plates with due solemnity, and the party settles to supper.

G.   Now Clown sees his chance. He runs ridiculously to centre and beckons to Pantaloon to join him, and up waddles Pantaloon, wondering what Joey is up to now. Clown has an idea, which he expounds laboriously.
  ' You and I will give them some of that Vin d'Arlequin, and then *they* will fall asleep, and . . . well . . . see ? '
  Pantaloon is slow to pick up the idea, but he sees Clown's mouth opening prodigiously. It's evidently a joke. Vin d'Arlequin, the magic wine of the Immortals . . . they'll fall asleep. . . . Priscilla could be stolen away. . . . Ah ! He . . . he sees it. And off he goes into crows and cackles and side-splitting paroxysms of laughter with Clown.

H.   Then suddenly, with two simultaneous and ridiculous jumps, they turn, face the sideboard, run up to it, and pick up two bottles of wine. They run across to the table and pour out glasses for George and the two aunts, one of whom lays a forbidding hand on Priscilla's glass, signifying that she is too young for wine. Priscilla pouts. *She,* a married woman ; but Clown winks at her, and she half guesses a joke, while George and the aunts raise their glasses, drink a little, and replace the glasses on the table, with strange sighs of unusual contentment and well-being.

I.   Priscilla looks at them hopefully. Perhaps they will cheer up after all. But, to her amazement, their highly respectable heads begin to nod. Each in turn makes a heroic effort to wake up, and looks reprovingly at the other heads sinking swiftly into unconsciousness. But their efforts are unavailing, and in a moment or two the scandal is complete—George and his aunts are fast asleep at the supper-table.

Priscilla is near to tears again. Oh ! how dull they are. But there is her little tune singing in her ears once more, so she rises from the table, and rather sadly begins a few steps of a dreamy dance.

But, oh ! It's so dull always dancing alone, and she breaks off disconsolately. Clown and Pantaloon are watching and listening eagerly. Will they come, Harlequin and Pierrot, her immortal lovers, and steal back again the lonely Columbine lost in a desert of respectability ? It's an anxious moment, but their plot has succeeded well so far.

Priscilla is now sitting in a disconsolate heap, dreaming by the fire.

J. Surely ? Yes, the lights are turning blue for the moonlight of a dream, the curtains at the back are parted, and there, waiting outside, is—Pierrot. Priscilla's figure, lit by the warm glow of the fire, seems to shed its Victorian primness ; the flickering flames hide flowers in her hair, her face and hands are like flowers too. Her eyes are starry. Once more she is Columbine.

Pierrot stands a moment in the centre opening. He is all that Pierrot should be—dreamy, poetical. In his hand he holds his pen and book, and waits poised to catch the song that is ever singing in his head. Then he sees Priscilla, and all his love of long ago flows back to him. Priscilla, half a-dream, rises from before the fire, and sees Pierrot. Her heart gives just that flutter it always did when Pierrot made poems for her in the moonlight in France in some other life. She flies away down right, all a-flutter with excitement. Pierrot follows her, and in a moment he is on his knees beside her, and writing another verse to his immortal love song. Then he speaks to her, saying :

' You are the lady of my poem——''

Priscilla is in more of a flutter than ever. She had always, in secret, wanted George to write a poem for her. But George only wrote cheques for the housekeeping, and there's no poetry in cheques.

Pierrot puts into her hand the poem he has written, and she reads it, thrilling at the words she had always longed to hear. Pierrot falls in a dream, however, at the sight of her flower-like hands touching his poem, and wanders away to the fire to compose a ' Sonnet to My Lady's Hands ', and promptly forgets all about Priscilla herself. Clown and Pantaloon are disappointed in him, but that's always the trouble with Pierrot, he does wander so terribly between inspiration and practicality.

K. But what matter ? Here's Harlequin, all a-shimmer with silver spangles, smiling behind his black mask, gallant, irresistible. He sweeps down to Priscilla, where she stands as Pierrot left her, and she turns to find Harlequin bowing beside her. And Harlequin is such a disturbing person. Memories of Mount Olympus, thousands of years ago, of Italy, and of Drury Lane at Christmas-time seem to throng about her. Harlequin is kissing her hand. (And George had forgotten her birthday.) Now Harlequin gives her a lovely red rose, and everybody knows what *that* means. (And George threw away the one she gave him.)

Priscilla is all Columbine now. She floats away to centre with her love-gifts, Pierrot's poem, and Harlequin's rose, and stands with outstretched arms—a butterfly poised for flight, a little wife half-afraid, half-entranced, and the moonlight from somewhere or other touches her as it did in the old pantomime days of ' Limes '.

She can't see Harlequin, because she daren't look, but she can feel him drawing nearer and nearer. Then he is on his knees beside her, and saying, as only Harlequin *can* say it, ' I love you.'

At last Priscilla looks down at him and half-hesitatingly holds out her hand. But as he touches it she remembers Pierrot, dreaming by the fire. She slips away to him and touches him on the shoulder. He follows her as she runs back to Harlequin, and he falls on his knee on the other side of her. Hardly conscious of what she is doing, but radiant

4

with excitement, Priscilla holds out a hand to each, and as the lovers bend to kiss the hands of Columbine, Clown and Pantaloon steal up behind, and, unseen, extend their hands in absurd benediction over the Immortal Lovers reunited in Bayswater.

L.   But there's many a slip, and Columbine is not won back to them yet. At the critical moment George gives vent to a shattering and resounding sneeze. The dream is broken. Pierrot and Harlequin fade into the shadows as the moonlight gives place to the comfortable glow of a Bayswater dining-room. Clown and Pantaloon are servants once more. George, still only half-awakened, is wrestling with another threatening sneeze. He has one of his colds. And Priscilla, bewildered and rather conscience-stricken, wonders how she can have dreamed so realistically as to be left with a tell-tale poem and rose in her hands. She thrusts them hastily into her dress and rushes to George. He needs careful management when he has a cold ! At the moment he is ravaged by incipient sneezes, and, handkerchief to nose, he gropes blindly towards the sofa and the fire, led by Priscilla, all wifely solicitude. He finally sinks upon the sofa as the culminating sneeze explodes. There he sits the picture of suffering, the very personification of a cold in the head. Priscilla in desperation runs to the aunts and rouses them from the effects of their sleep and implores their assistance.

M.   They rise to their feet and to the occasion. ' George has a cold ; we have warned him so often about changing his underwear so early in the Spring.'
      They sail down centre and regard the pitiable object he presents, and tap their noses significantly. Priscilla, meanwhile, retreats down right and tries to collect her scattered wits.
      The aunts, turning simultaneously, sail to the sideboard and return to the sofa with cold-remedies. The First Aunt stands behind George with a woollen muffler, the Second stands centre with a large green bottle.
      The scarf is wound round and round the throat of the

protesting George, the bottle is thrust beneath his nose, but, after one sniff, he waves it weakly away. The aunts stand centre, and the First Aunt says, ' George, go upstairs to bed.' George assents, and totters to centre between them, forming a little procession facing the door up left. George waves a hand, as if to say, ' Lead on ; it is a far, far better thing to go to bed.' The aunts sign to Priscilla to follow. Clown and Pantaloon miserably place candles in their hands as the aunts pass them, and the procession leaves the dining-room, and we hear George's last and most excruciating sneeze as he mounts the stairs. Priscilla stops centre, too bewildered to move. Her dream was so beautiful, and so suddenly shattered, she wonders if it can really have happened. Clown and Pantaloon look dejectedly round, wondering if there's any hope after all.

N. But now the light is turning to dreams and moonlight once more. And there is the little tune Pierrot and Columbine found in France : ' Au Claire de la Lune, mon ami Pierrot ' ; and as Priscilla feels for her rose and her poem, sure enough Harlequin and Pierrot steal out of the shadows again. This time Priscilla *dare* not look at them. She stands clasping her poem and her rose to her beating heart, with her eyes seeing, far, far down the centuries, all the dreams of love that have been hers. Harlequin and Pierrot are drawing nearer and nearer. Once more they kneel beside her. Once more Clown and Pantaloon creep up behind. Surely they have caught their Columbine after all. In another minute she must look at her lovers, and then she'll be away with them, far, far from marriage and Bayswater and George and cheques, when—George, in the distance, sneezes yet again, and the spell is broken.

But Priscilla has understood. The Immortals have called to Columbine, but she cannot go. She is held in Bayswater by something stronger than dreams and flowers. She is bound to George by wifely affection.

O. Yet for a moment she laughs as Columbine laughed of old, and tearing off one little red shoe, she flings it high into the air above the heads of Harlequin and Pierrot. Something of her is always theirs, she will never forget ; but as they catch the little red shoe of Columbine, Priscilla runs away to minister to the needs of her lawful husband George.

Harlequin and Pierrot slip into the moonlit opening, centre back, and raise aloft Priscilla's shoe, their memory of Columbine, where the moonlight haloes it with dreams. Clown springs to attention, a butler once more, and Pantaloon, unable to resist a joke, crawls under the table and peers from under the table-cloth at the closing scene. Clown can hardly resist saying, ' 'Ullo, old 'un,' to him, but refrains, as Priscilla appears once more.

P.   This time she leads George, swathed to the eyes in wraps and leaning on a stick, to the sofa by the fire. There she installs him comfortably. She knows he really enjoys a good ' fussing ' when he has a cold, and she *does* love to take care of somebody, and to be *needed*. Somehow the shadows of the firelit room are fraught with strange possibilities, and her one shoeless foot, which will protrude itself, has to be thrust beneath her crinoline. But the dreams are fading. The room is filled with the notes of the old song ' Home, Sweet Home ', and, after all, George is a dear old thing. Part of her will always live as Columbine with the Immortals ; there will always be a dance in her feet, but as she slips to the ground beside George, and he forgets his cold enough to find comfort in putting his arm about her, she realizes that in her heart Priscilla, the prim little wife, loves her perfectly Victorian husband.

The curtain falls on a picture that leaves Pantaloon shaking his head at the failure of their plot to recapture Columbine.

NOTES ON MUSIC

Music Required :

Menuet (from *Nordiska*, Book III)	F. Rung
Noah's Ark	A. Roloff
Moments Musicaux. Opus 84. No. 4 in G. ..	Moszkowski

(Published by Augener & Co., Ltd.)

A Dream Garden .. .. J. Morel

(Published by Walsh & Co.)

Old Songs : *Au Clair de la Lune*
Home, Sweet Home

A. *Menuet.* F. Rung. *Entrance of Aunts*

Play 16 bars and repeat them

Entrance of First Aunt	4 bars
Entrance of Second Aunt	4 bars
Both move down left and sit	8 bars

On Repeat :

They get out their knitting and knit	8 bars
First Aunt : ' She has been dancing '	4 bars
Second Aunt speaks : ' She has been showing her ankles '	4 bars

B. *A Dream Garden.* No. 4. Morel.

Entrance of Priscilla, Clown, and Pantaloon

Entrance of Priscilla. She puts down her flowers and calls Clown and Pantaloon	16 bars
Entrance of Clown and Pantaloon	8 bars
Priscilla arranges her flowers, runs and kisses the First Aunt	8 bars
Priscilla begins to dance	8 bars
She goes to Clown, waltzes with him ; they bump into the sofa	8 bars
First Aunt speaks : ' You must not dance any more '	4 bars
Second Aunt speaks : ' You must not show your ankles '	4 bars
Priscilla speaks : ' I am not to dance ? Oh, very well ! '	8 bars
She finishes arranging the table and goes down right to wait for George. Clown and Pantaloon stand up centre	16 bars

C. *Menuet.* F. Rung. *Entrance of George*

Begin at bar 17 ; play 20 bars. Play 8 bars and repeat
them. Play 16 bars

Introduction	2 bars
Entrance of George; he bows to the Aunts ..	14 bars

Priscilla goes and kisses him .. .. .. 4 bars
First Aunt rises and says : ' Listen to me ' .. 4 bars
Second Aunt rises and says : ' Listen to me ' .. 4 bars

On Repeat :

First Aunt : ' She has been dancing again ' .. 4 bars
Second Aunt : ' She has been showing her ankles ' 4 bars
George : ' Have you been dancing ? ' .. .. 4 bars
Priscilla : ' Yes, I have ! ' .. .. 4 bars
George : ' You must not dance any more ' .. 4 bars
Priscilla crosses to George, stamps and runs down
    right .. .. 4 bars

D. *Noah's Ark.* Roloff. ' The Elephant.'   *The Supper*
Entrance of Clown and Pantaloon with the dishes 8 bars
They take off the covers and come to centre .. 4 bars
They say : ' Supper is served ! ' .. .. .. 4 bars

E. *Noah's Ark.* Roloff. ' The Cuckoo.'   *The Supper (con.)*
Priscilla takes the Aunts to the table and they sit 12 bars
Priscilla takes George to the table and they sit 13 bars

F. *Noah's Ark.* Roloff. ' The Elephant.'   *The Supper (con.)*
George carves the first plate .. .. .. 4 bars
George carves the second plate .. .. .. 4 bars
George carves the third plate .. .. .. 4 bars
George carves the fourth plate .. .. .. 4 bars

G. *Noah's Ark.* Roloff. ' The Lion.'   *The Supper (con.)*
Clown comes to centre and calls Pantaloon .. 6 bars
Clown says : ' I will give them a drink, which will
    send them to sleep ' .. .. 8 bars
    They both laugh .. .. 4 bars

H. *Noah's Ark.* Roloff. ' The Tiger.'   *The Supper (con.)*
Clown and Pantaloon turn .. .. .. 1 bar
They fetch the wine and pour it out .. .. 4 bars
The Aunts and George drink and begin to feel
    drowsy .. .. 4 bars

I. *A Dream Garden.* No. 4. Morel.
Play 32 bars

Priscilla watches the family fall asleep and gets up   16 bars
She begins to dance, breaks off, and goes to the fire   16 bars

J.   *A Dream Garden.* No. 2. Morel.   *Pierrot*

Play through and repeat

Entrance of Pierrot ..   ..   15 bars
Priscilla runs to down right. Pierrot follows and
     kneels   ..   ..   8 bars

On Repeat.

Pierrot says : ' I write a poem. You are the lady
     in my poem '   ..   ..   8 bars
He gives it to her   ..   ..   7 bars
She reads it and puts it in her dress. He wanders
     to the fire   ..   ..   8 bars

K.   *A Dream Garden.* No. 1. Morel.   *Harlequin*

Entrance of Harlequin. He bows to Priscilla   ..   8 bars
He kisses her hand and gives her a rose   ..   ..   8 bars
Columbine runs to centre, holding the rose and poem   16 bars
Harlequin kneels to her   ..   ..   4 bars
He says : ' I love you,' and kisses her hand   ..   8 bars
Priscilla fetches Pierrot They kneel one on each
     side of her. On the last chord George sneezes   8 bars

L.   *Menuet.* F. Rung.   *George's Cold*

Begin at bar 37 ; play 8 bars and repeat them. Play 16 bars.
Pierrot and Harlequin run down right and left   ..   8 bars

On Repeat.

George sneezes again. Priscilla runs to him   ..   8 bars
He gets up and they go to the fire. On the last
     chord he sits on the sofa with another sneeze   16 bars

M.   *Moments Musicaux.* No. 4. Moszkowski.

The Remedies and Exeunt Aunts and George

Play 9 bars. Cut 6 bars. Play to end

The Aunts come down and look at George   ..   5 bars
They say to each other : ' He has a cold '   ..   4 bars
They fetch the bottle and the scarf   ..   ..   10 bars
First Aunt puts the scarf round his neck ..   ..   4 bars
Second Aunt puts the bottle under his nose   ..   4 bars

First Aunt says : ' George, go to bed ' .. .. 2 bars
They form a procession and exeunt .. .. 10 bars

N. *Au Clair de la Lune,*   *Priscilla's Dream Again*
                         16 bars
Pierrot and Harlequin come back. Clown and
Pantaloon come down and stand behind
Priscilla. On the last note George sneezes .. 16 bars

O. *A Dream Garden.* No. 4. Morel. *Priscilla leaves the Immortals*
                Play the last 16 bars
Priscilla takes off her shoe and throws it to Harle-
quin and Pierrot. They take it up centre.
Priscilla runs off
Clown goes and stands by the sofa. Pantaloon
goes under the table .. .. 16 bars

P. *Home, Sweet Home.*
                    16 bars
Priscilla and George come back to the fire. George
sits on the sofa and Priscilla on the floor beside
him .. .. 16 bars

FURNITURE

Stage :
Victorian dining-table.
4 chairs.
Plush- or leather-covered sofa with a Paisley shawl or an
antimacassar on the back of it.
Sideboard.

PROPERTY PLOT

On table, up right :
White cloth
4 wine-glasses.
2 chairs above table.
1 chair at right end of table.
1 chair at left end of table.

On Sideboard, up left :
2 wine-bottles.

2 candles in brass candlesticks.
Box of matches.
Medicine bottle.
Scarf.

Off Stage, left :

Hat					
Stick	}	..	..	..	*George*
Dressing-gown					
2 workbags containing knitting	..		..	..	*Aunts*
Bouquet with one loose flower	..		..	..	*Priscilla*
Tray with 4 knives, 4 forks		..	..	..	*Clown*
Meat Pie under dish-cover		..	..	..	*Ditto*
Cruet	.. .. ..	..	..	..	*Pantaloon*
4 plates	.. .. ..	..	..	..	*Ditto*

Off Centre :

2 letters	.. .. ..	..	..	..	*Pierrot*
Quill pen	.. .. ..	..	..	..	*Ditto*
Rose	.. .. ..	..	..	..	*Harlequin*

COSTUME

First and Secon d Aunts :

Crinoline of about 1864 (i.e. with a big hoop).
The bodice cut with a high neck and finished with a cream or
  white neckband.
Long, rather full, sleeves.
The whole dress carried out, one in black or black and white
  very small check taffeta or fine woollen material ; the
  other in plum colour or dark bottle green.
Paisley or black lace shawls may be worn.
Black cotton stockings.
Black flat-heeled shoes.
Hair : Either parted in the centre, or taken straight back off
  the forehead and plaited into a ' door-knocker ' and encased
  in a chenille net.

Priscilla :

Crinoline cut low in the neck and worn ' off ' the shoulders
  with short puff sleeves.

The bodice well boned and tight-fitting and cut to a point in front.

The dress carried out in a delicate colour in taffeta or heavy silk.

White stockings.

Unblocked satin ballet shoes, scarlet.

Hair : Parted in the centre, plaited into a ' door-knocker '' and a wreath of small flowers to tone with the dress worn well back on the head.

CLOWN, PANTALOON AND HARLEQUIN
IN A VICTORIAN PANTOMIME
(*From ' Punch ', 1859*)

George :

Buff or grey peg-top trousers.

Blue or black coat.

Frilled shirt.

Stock.

Top-hat.

Hair parted at the side and brushed up in front.
Mutton-chop whiskers.

Clown and Pantaloon :
  Footmen's dress with knee-breeches and frogged coats.
  Clown and Pantaloon wigs and make-up.

Pierrot :
  White Pierrot dress with white ruff and black skull-cap.
  White stockings and white unblocked ballet shoes.
  White make-up.

Harlequin :
  Spangle Harlequin dress.
  Black ruff.
  Black skull-cap.
  Belt and pouch.
  Black satin cloak.

LES ANGÉLUS DU PRINTEMPS

(Music by Paul de Maleingreau.)

LES ANGÉLUS DU PRINTEMPS

It is the month of May, when strange things are stirring and strange feelings waken in most unexpected bosoms.

The Scene is the square of a small town in Southern France. A flight of steps leads into a church up left. At the centre back is the door of a house, above it a curtained window.

It is the dawn of May Day, when the children and young girls bring flowers and lighted candles in a procession to the church in the village square. It is also the dawn of market day, when the vegetable and flower stalls are bright with country produce, and the little ladies and gentlemen of the town go a-marketing.

The characters are :

THE WANDERING IMMORTALS

Pierrot	..	..	..	.. ⎱ *The Spirits of Love*
Columbine	..	..	..	.. ⎰ *and Beauty*
Scaramouche		..	..	.. *The Spirit of Comedy*

MORTALS

The Beadle
The Market Woman
A Country Maidservant
A Young Peasant
Country Men and Women
Townspeople, Ladies and Gentlemen
Children
Nursemaids

SCENE I

L'Angélus du Matin

The village square is wrapt almost in darkness.

As the curtain rises, Pierrot, Columbine and Scaramouche are discovered as shadowy figures, asleep, leaning against each other, down left. They wandered into the town the night before, and, being unable to find a lodging, slept in the square. At the back a bulky form leans against a wall, also asleep. It is the Beadle.

A faint sound of the Angelus bell is heard, and the first dim light of the dawn grows. The Beadle wakes with a start, and jangles his bell, a little peevishly ; these dawns are cold, even in May.

The light grows a little more, and Pierrot and Columbine wake gradually. They yawn and stretch, stand up and greet each other rather sleepily. Scaramouche wakes with a grunt ; he is none too good-tempered in the early morning.

The Beadle rings his bell more noisily.

From up left and down right the country people begin to arrive with their produce of flowers and fruit. The Market Woman is with them. They are tired and sleepy with their walk in the darkness from the fields where they gathered their wares. But as the light grows they become more animated. The Young Peasant and the Maidservant are with them. She goes into a house door, at centre back, and blows a kiss to him as she disappears.

Some one points to where the sky is brightening each moment ; they must get on with their work, to be ready in the market at sunrise.

Suddenly, they see the Immortals in their midst. These disreputable players again ! The Beadle rings his bell furiously, bidding them begone. They plead to be allowed to stay in the town for May Day. Columbine says that she has brought her flowers for the May Day procession, but the Beadle is adamant.

Reluctantly, and a little sadly, the players wander away and out of sight up left. But something tells us that we shall see them again. It takes more than a Beadle to discourage the Immortals.

Now there is a bustle among the country people. Some go off up right, and return with a wooden table ; others bring poles and a brightly-coloured awning. In a moment the flower and vegetable stall is set up, in another it is bright with country flowers and fruit, and the Market Woman is seated beside it under her striped umbrella, her knitting in her hand.

Again some one points to the sky. The sunrise at last. May Day is dawning. The men stand bare-headed as the sun rises in its full glory and floods the little square with light. Gaiety is everywhere at last ; the world is awake.

Sounds of a procession are heard approaching, and a band of children and young girls in white dresses appears, each carrying a bunch of spring flowers and a lighted candle. It is the May Day procession of the children, headed by a boy carrying a pole decked with greenery, flowers, and ribbons. The procession passes up the steps into the church. The little town is ready for the work and play of the day.

The morning Angelus is passed.

(The curtains close for a moment to denote the passing
of the hours.)

B.

Scene II

MATINÉE (PROMENADE)
Folâtreries dans la Rosée

It is the middle of the morning. The ladies of the town arrive to do their shopping in the market-place. They are prim little figures, carrying baskets and reticules. With them are those dear old gentlemen and crusty colonels who inhabit quiet country towns.

They approach the Market Woman, inquire the price of flowers and vegetables this morning. A little pleasant bargaining is taking place, when a queer sound of piping is heard. The bargaining stops abruptly.

The piping continues, and we see that it is Pierrot. He has a shepherd's pipe, and is playing a wicked jaunty tune. Dancing to himself and calling the prim little townspeople away from their neat little lives to some memory of dancing on dewy lawns on May Days long ago.

Their feet begin absurdly halting dance steps, and each picks up some flowers or a vegetable from the stall and, with it, begins a rather formal and prim little dance. Their joints are stiff ; they are unaccustomed to dancing in any form, let

5

alone a Maytime dance with flowers and fruit, but the piping goes on, and in spite of themselves they continue to dance until they are in a circle. The Beadle and the Market Woman, rather ponderously, join in.

Into the middle of the circle flits a white figure, like a flying dove : it is Columbine poised airily. Now Pierrot is beside her. And he tells her the old, old story of the spring, the one that begins ' I love you.'

Something thrills the prim little ladies ; they step coyly out of the circle and stand waiting in something of a flutter.

The little old gentlemen and the colonels follow them with jaunty steps, and, falling upon their knees, repeat the old, old story, ' I love you.'

Columbine and Pierrot flit among the couples, spreading magic wherever they go. Then suddenly they disappear, off up left, behind the church.

The ladies and gentlemen tread a sprightly dance together, which somehow leads them to surround the Beadle and the Market Woman, and he, kneeling a trifle painfully beside her, declares more sonorously than them all, ' I love you.'

Suddenly the piping ceases. The little ladies, the old gentlemen and the colonels, the Beadle and the Market Woman are dumbfounded. How came they into these unseemly situations ? Surreptitiously each one places the flowers or fruit into his or her shopping-bag. The Market Woman returns to her seat, the Beadle to his place beside the church steps. Every one hopes that no one noticed his or her inexplicable lapse from decorum. There must be something odd in the air of the first of May.

Primly and self-consciously they disappear off right to finish the day's shopping in a less dangerous locality.

The Beadle goes on his round, the Market Woman knits a trifle feverishly.

Columbine and Pierrot steal on together, hand in hand, delighted at the success of their prank upon the town that tried to turn away the Immortals.

Then they, too, disappear.

(And again for a moment the curtains close.)

SCARAMOUCHE
IN ' LES ANGÉLUS DU PRINTEMPS '

C.

L'Angélus de Midi

(L'Ardente Sérénade)

The square is golden with midday sun, and empty. The sound of a guitar is heard, and there enters, from up right, Scaramouche, playing a serenade, swaggering, gallant, and distinctly disreputable.

He circles the stage and then places himself beneath the window. His song grows more alluring, and, surely enough, the curtains part, and there looks out the rosy face of the comely Country Maidservant. Scaramouche ceases his song, speaks to her, and begs her to come down to him, telling her how pretty she is.

But now there enters, angrily, the Young Peasant. What is this vulgar player doing making love to his little sweetheart? He will box his ears for him! They are about to set upon each other when the midday Angelus sounds. They cease; the peasant boy pulls off his cap and stands with bowed head. Scaramouche waits a moment, and then makes a tactful and unostentatious exit up right. He simply is not there when the peasant looks up again to continue the fight which the Angelus interrupted.

The hidden girl looks out once more. She sees below her own sweetheart, not the strange swaggering gallant who was making love to her a moment before. She disappears, and then trips out of the door of the house to him. In a moment they are gone together.

Once more Scaramouche's haunting tune is heard, and back he comes, smiling to himself, swaggering still, and wanders on out of sight up left. There are other windows, and France is full of pretty little maids, ready to hear his serenades in the lazy noontide sunlight.

(The curtains close.)

D.

Scene IV

Berceuse d'Après-midi

It is afternoon, the time of siesta; sleep is beginning to steal over the quiet town. There enter four neat little nurse-maids, carrying four neat little babies from up left. They walk sedately and carefully, and rock their charges, until they whisper, ' Hush ! He is asleep.'

The children, too, are tired of their May Day games. They enter, also from left, sleepily humming a nursery rhyme, and seat themselves on the ground, leaning against each other. ' You and I must go to sleep,' they sing. ' This eye and that is closing.' ' You and I are going to sleep.' And they rock themselves a moment and are asleep.

Pierrot and Columbine wander on, also humming a little sleepy song. They kiss like two children, slide to the ground back to back, rocking to and fro against each other. The Market Woman nods. The children nod, the nursemaids nod as they rock the sleeping babies. And, at the back, the Beadle nods majestically—until, as the rocking-tune dies away, sleep gathers them all.

(The curtains close.)

E.

Scene V

L'Angélus du Soir

(Prélude—Hymne—Crépuscule)

The sun has left the square. Evening has come. The Beadle enters from up left to centre. The peasants return wearily from their work, or May Day celebrations, and slowly mount the steps into the church, passing across the stage from up right. They are heavy-footed in the evening. The Beadle takes up his position beside the church steps. The little ladies pass also towards the church, whence the ghost of a hymn comes out. More peasants follow, and the old gentlemen also go into the church for the evening service ; and, lastly, the Beadle mounts the steps and disappears. When all are there we hear the organ playing. The Market Woman is left listening, crossing herself as she hears the sound of the service coming from within the church.

The music swells and the sound of the hymn pours out into the evening air. At its climax the children come out in procession. The May Day service and celebrations are over. The townspeople and peasants, too, pour out of the church, and as the sunset light gilds the square, it is full of people, a gay and happy scene.

For a moment a queer little tune is heard once more, and suddenly at the top of the steps, lit by the light of the sinking sun, stand the three Immortals, looking down on the quiet town they have visited for a brief day.

But dusk is falling. Mysterious shadows begin to wrap the square. The bright colours fade and the human people slip away into the gathering darkness. Homes call when evening comes. No one is left in the square.

No one ? Yes, the three wandering Immortals are there, still forgotten of men, and in the gloaming some strange radiance seems shed about them : the radiance of the old magic, perhaps. They leave the church steps and come to the centre of the square.

A horn sounds faintly in the distance. Pierrot recognizes the call. He bids his fellow-travellers pass on with him. There are other towns to visit with the Spirits of Love and Laughter. It may be a long road. But it is a gay road. It seems as if some vision leads them as they pass out. And the Angelus becomes a carillon of far and faery bells, ringing down the ages, calling into the Future : the Angelus of the Eternal Spring.

(The curtains close for the last time.)

NOTES ON MUSIC

Music Required :

Les Angélus du Printemps .. .. Paul de Maleingreau
(Published by J. & W. Chester, Ltd.)

A. *L'Angélus du Matin.*

The Immortals sleep	4 bars
The Beadle's bell	3 bars
Columbine and Pierrot wake, then Scaramouche ..	12 bars
The Beadle's bell	2 bars
Entrance of peasants..	11 bars
The Beadle tells Immortals to be gone	4 bars
They plead to stay	4 bars
They exeunt, followed by Beadle	8 bars
Two peasants exeunt to fetch stall	2 bars
Do. do.	2 bars
Do. do.	4 bars
Re-enter with table	2 bars
Re-enter with poles	3 bars
Re-enter with canopy. Arrange stall, bring vegetables, etc. Market Woman settles herself ..	8 bars
All in position waiting sunrise	5 bars
The procession	16 bars

B. *Matinée.*

Entrance of ladies to stall	5 bars
Entrance of gentlemen	3 bars
Conversation and bargaining	4 bars
Entrance of Beadle	2 bars
All collect purchases	2 bars
Pierrot plays his pipe and appears down left ; crosses down right. Ladies and gentlemen feel something queer is happening	12 bars
Ladies and gentlemen dance and form a circle ..	12 bars
Columbine runs in to centre from up left	3 bars
Pierrot's declaration of love	4 bars
Ladies look at gentlemen, who kneel	8 bars
Gentlemen's declaration	5 bars
Pierrot and Columbine run among them and exeunt	6 bars

Ladies and gentlemen dance in couples	12 bars
Beadle and Market Woman down to centre ..	4 bars
Beadle's declaration of love	5 bars
They all recover themselves and exeunt	12 bars
Pierrot and Columbine return and exeunt again	5 bars

C. *L'Angélus de Midi.*

Scaramouche enters and goes down left, playing..	10 bars
He turns up centre	4 bars
He calls up to the window	4 bars
The girl looks out	4 bars
He says : ' You come down. You are pretty ' ..	8 bars
The Peasant Boy enters and threatens Scaramouche	8 bars
Midday bell. Scaramouche and boy still. Then exit Scaramouche	7 bars
The boy turns. The girl looks out. Comes down. Exeunt	5 bars
Re-entrance and exit of Scaramouche	14 bars

D. *Berceuse d'Après-midi.*

Entrance of nursemaids, rocking babies	11 bars
Entrance of children and sit	8 bars
' You and I go to sleep, this eye that eye closes. You and I go to sleep.' Rock..	14 bars
Pierrot and Columbine enter, kiss, sit and rock ..	6 bars
Market Woman sleeps, and they all rock	5 bars

E. *L'Angélus du Soir.*

Enter Beadle	5 bars
Enter peasants and into church	8 bars
Beadle moves down	5 bars
More peasants	6 bars
Ladies and gentlemen enter and into church ..	3 bars
Beadle up and into Church	6 bars
The hymn ; Market Woman listens	6 bars
Children out, followed by crowd	5 bars
Immortals appear on steps	3 bars
Crowd moves about and gradually disappears ..	6 bars
Immortals to centre	2 bars
They hear the call. Pierrot points the way. They hear the echo and go	13 bars

PROPERTY PLOT

Stage :

Flight of steps leading into church half up left. Rostrum and steps leading off.

Off Up Right :

Wooden table, with slots for poles.
4 wooden poles.
Striped awning.
Baskets of vegetables and fruit.
Stool.

Hand :

Bell ..	..	..	..	.. *Beadle*
Knitting ..	..	..	..	.. *Market Woman*
Guitar ..	..	..	..	.. *Scaramouche*
Flowers ..	..	..	..	.. *Columbine*
Flowers ..	..	..	..	.. *Children*
Lighted candles ..	..	..	..	.. *Ditto*
Shopping baskets ..	..	..	..	.. *Ladies and Gentlemen*
Shepherd's pipe ..	..	..	..	.. *Pierrot*
4 Babies ..	..	..	..	.. *Nursemaids*

COSTUME

Pierrot :

White Pierrot suit (trousers and loose coat).
Ruffle.
Skull-cap.
White stockings and shoes.
White make-up.

Columbine :

Tarlatan ballet dress (white), with fitting bodice ; skirt ankle length.
Tights.
Ballet shoes.
Wreath of roses.

Scaramouche :

Black knee-breeches.
Black jacket fastening down front (buttoned).
Leather sword-belt (with or without sword).

Small white ruffle.
Black circular cloak, knee length.
Soft cap like a tam-o'-shanter, pleated into a band round head.
Black stockings.
Heeled shoes with large rosettes.
White make-up with small moustache and tiny pointed beard on chin.
(Scaramouche is really a masked character, but make-up will probably prove more satisfactory.)

Beadle :

Dark blue knee-breeches.
Red coat, skirted and caped, with large side-pockets.
White waistcoat.
Cocked hat.
White cotton or woollen stockings.
Black buckled shoes.
(See Dickens : *Sketches by Boz.*)

Market Woman :

Full red skirt to ground, dark blue apron.
Fitting bodice.
Small black woollen shawl crossed over chest.
Coloured handkerchief tied under hair behind, or under chin.
White stockings.
Black shoes, heavy and flat-heeled.

Peasant Women :

Full, long, coloured skirts, aprons.
White or coloured blouses.
Cross-over shawls.
Handkerchiefs on head, some with white head handkerchiefs tied under chin, below wide, low-crowned, straw hats. Some lace caps.
White stockings.
Black shoes.

Peasant Men :

Dark blue trousers.
Blue blouse shirts, belted.
Handkerchief at neck.
Soft caps, or rather wide felt hats.

Coloured socks.
Heavy dark shoes.

Nursemaids :

Long coloured print dresses, with fitting bodices.
Large white aprons, with bib, and ends tied behind and hanging
down.
White caps with streamers, or big black bows on the top of the
head, with long streamers.
White stockings.
Black buttoned boots.

Children :

Full white muslin dresses.
Coloured sashes.
Hair ribbons.
White stockings.
Black shoes.

Boy :

Brown knickers.
White shirt.
Stockings and shoes.

Ladies :

Walking costume, 1812-20 (or the 'seventies, if preferred).
Dresses, high-waisted, long, tight sleeves.
Short-waisted jackets, or short capes.
Skirts straight and clinging.
Flowered bonnets, or hats tied under chin.
Sunshades.
Light stockings.
Flat sandal shoes.

Gentlemen :

Buff breeches, tight-fitting to below knee, or close-fitting
trousers, 1812–20.
Tail coats, dull red or brown, double-breasted, with high collar.
Light waistcoats, striped or flowered.
Frilled shirts.
White stockings.
Black pumps.
Top-hats.

Printed in the USA
CPSIA information can be obtained
at www.ICGtesting.com
LVHW040208070224
771196LV00006B/130

9 781447 452409